Ernest Jones'

# SWING

## THE

# CLUBHEAD

## METHOD

Ernest Jones'
# SWING
## THE
# CLUBHEAD
## METHOD

FIRST EDITION 1937

Skylane
PUBLISHING

Library of Congress Control Number: 2004110190

ISBN: 0-9760174-0-7

Skylane Publishing
P.O. Box 2129
Sparks, NV  89432

Printed in The United States of America

# CONTENTS

# FOREWARD

Ernest Jones was one of Great Britain's top young players. During World War I, Ernest lost one of his legs, ending his tournament career. He then turned his focus to teaching - becoming the most sought after teacher in golfing history. From 1924 - 1960, he taught in the United States as the Professional at the Women's National Golf Club on Long Island and then worked out of an indoor studio in Manhattan. It is well known that he gave over 3,000 lessons a year and created over a dozen Major Championship winners and numerous Club and Regional Champions. Ernest was honored when inducted into the World Golf Hall of Fame and was voted "... *top teachers of all-time.*" (Golf Magazine, Feb. 1998)

Ernests' teaching genius was based on Universal Laws of Science and simple logic. Galileo's discovery of the isochronism of the pendulum laid the foundation. Leonardo DaVinci's work on force was all Jones needed to put a true golf swing into place.

Galileo's work teaches us: It takes the same time to complete a small arc as a large one, providing you use the same length of shaft. Accordingly, they will have the same feel. Davinci said: *"A blow is the son of motion, the grandson of force, whilst their mutual ancestor is weight."* Translation - a blow is striking the golf ball; the motion is a swinging motion; force is centrifugal force; and the weight is the clubhead.

Jones realized, you couldn't have a swing unless you have the motion of a swing in the clubhead. Furthermore, you couldn't dissect motion into parts and still have motion: therefore, it is impossible to take a swing apart and still have a swing. The great Bobby Jones, (no relation to Ernest) endorsed Ernest and said: *"... we in the PGA picture tend to take a swing apart and divide it into parts, but we know you can't teach it that way."* You see, a swing is one continuous to-and-fro motion, which repeats between the same place. Watch the pendulum in a Grandfather clock, or a child swinging in a park, and you will see a to-and-fro motion.

Ernest taught the **feel** of a true swinging motion, sensing it through the hands - that correct mechanics follow automatically. In his own words: *"The hands are the medium which controls the swing, with body parts - arms, legs, shoulders and such - performing as admirable followers."* Today, golf instruction is poor at best, based on swing mechanics, rather than the feel of a true swing. All Professionals play by feel, but that's not how they teach! Some teach pure mechanics, while others combine mechanics and motion. Neither approach works effectively. *"In the last 25 years the handicap of the average golfer has remained the same."* (National Golf Foundation) The Jones method must be taught in its pure form, because it is based on Universal Laws. These Laws are absolute; you cannot change or make them better. To reiterate: you simply cannot change the feel or the laws that apply to a true swinging motion.

Chances are, if you don't swing the clubhead, a body part or position will go wrong. If you correct the body part or position, you are correcting the symptom, not the disease - correcting the effect, not the cause. Today, golf instruction is backwards. Gary Player stated: *"For every fundamental in golf, I will show you a superstar, and I don't use that word lightly, who doesn't do it."* It is sad, but with the exception of my brother, Arnie Frankel, I have yet to meet a professional that teaches the one and only thing that counts in a golf swing: THE MOTION IN THE CLUBHEAD AND THE FEEL OF A TRUE SWING.

Tour players do not understand a true swinging motion. Ben Hogan has this to say: *"I never know why I hit the ball well. I just know when I'm doing it."* Top players have the motion because of the countless hours of practice they put in, but when they lose the feel, they often go into major slumps. Many times, world-class golfers are never heard of again! This is truly one of golf's great tragedies.

Golfers, at every level, are blaming themselves instead of instruction that is not up to par. The golfer must be given the correct Key to unlock golf's great mystery. *"Swinging Into Golf"* gives you that key and stops the insanity of constant contradiction, positions and mechanical quick fixes that are here today and gone tomorrow.

By producing a swinging motion with the clubhead you will have:

{a} Rhythm and timing.

{b} Maximum acceleration at the bottom of the arc.

{c} A repeating arc = accuracy.

{d} Centrifugal force = distance.

{e} Balance.

What else can a golfer want? But in order to swing, you must accept the simplicity of the swing and learn to practice properly. Bobby Jones had it right when he said: *"The one idea for a golfer to always keep in mind is that, when playing a shot, his only job is to swing the clubhead. If he does this, striking the ball will take care of itself."*

The Ernest Jones' method produces a natural easier way to swing - reducing physical and mental strain - you only have to think of one thing when over a golf ball. Whether beginner or expert, you are guaranteed to benefit from this common sense approach. It's been said, *"common sense is not so common."* I pray this is not a true statement.

So go to it! SWING THE CLUBHEAD! Enjoy the greatest game the world has ever known.

Ron Frankel
Director of the Frankel Golf Academy

**Publisher's Note:**

The Frankel Golf Academy is the only school we are aware of that teaches the pure Ernest Jones method. For more information about the school or *Golf's One Motion Video Package*, visit them on the web at www.frankelgolf.com, or call 1-800-990-7761.

# INTRODUCTION

I began playing golf as a small boy near Manchester, England. At the age of eighteen, I received the appointment as assistant professional at the Chislehurst Golf Club on my qualifications as a good club maker and good player. I played a very creditable game, good enough, in fact, to qualify each time I entered the British Open Championship, in which I took part several times.

One of my duties as professional was to teach others to play. From my first effort, I realized that I had not the slightest idea of how to go about it. The situation was about the same as though I were being sent out to teach people how to throw stones. I could throw with reasonable accuracy, just as I could play golf quite well, but what then?

Something had to be done, so I decided that my best course was to begin a careful study of books on the game and how to teach it. I read books by the leading professionals, and many others besides, but I am frank to confess that, with a single exception, these, instead of helping me, merely added to my confusion, because of their many contradictions.

There was among these a volume, "The Art of Golf" by Sir Walter Simpson, published in 1887, which proved very helpful because it set me thinking along a line entirely different from anything I had encountered up to this time. It pointed out, among other things, that in golf "there is one categorical imperative, 'Hit the Ball,' but there are no minor absolutes."

This book emphasized the point that, while good players one and all, observe this one imperative, they differ, each from another, in the outward appearances of their actions. If that were true, then outward appearances were, after all, merely incidental. On that same theory, trying to teach golf by analyzing, bit by bit, successive movements in the stroke of a good player was an illogical procedure.

I still have a copy of "The Art of Golf," now long since out of print, and I treasure it highly. It marked the starting point for me in whatever success I have had at teaching the game. For that reason I hasten to give credit to it here and now.

Shortly after the outbreak of the World War, I joined the British army and was sent to France in November, 1915. In the fighting around Loos in March of the following year, I was badly wounded, and lost my right leg below the knee. Sent back to England, I was discharged from the hospital four months later. While still recuperating, I went back to golf. I was using crutches at the time, but in my first round I scored an 83 at Royal Norwich, and a bit later, playing with David Ayton, I scored 72 over the Clacton course, quite a long and testing layout.

I mention these personal experiences by way of showing that in spite of my physical handicap, which obviously must have changed the outward appearance of my stroke, I could still play well. This fact further confirmed me in my belief that the important essential in learning to play golf well is to accept the theory that the stroke must be regarded as one complete action, and to learn to put this theory into practice in wielding the club.

About this time I took part in several exhibition matches, and it was through these matches that I met Daryn Hammond, who wrote "The Golf Swing, the Ernest Jones Method," in which it was pointed out that the essence of the golf stroke is to have control of the club head through the hands and fingers. Twenty years of teaching this same principle has tended to prove and strenghten my faith in it. Playing golf is an art and not a science, and I have heard art defined as the science of elimination. So I have sought to eliminate other considerations and to stick to one principle, the art of swinging the club head.

I am speaking, of course, as a practical teacher. I have no quarrel with those who delight in analyzing the successive movements of different parts of the anatomy during the course of a stroke. Lots of us have a consuming curiosity to take a watch apart to see what makes it go. "The average golfer," to quote Sir Walter Simpson again, "must be allowed to theorize to some extent. It is a necessary concession to him as a thinking animal. . . On the other hand, if he does not recognize hitting the ball as his main business, and theory as a recreation, he becomes so bad a player that he nearly gives it up."

I think "Swing the club head" is preferable to "Hit the ball" because there are more ways than one of hitting it; a detailed discussion of this point will be found later in the text. And I claim nothing new or revolutionary in "Swing the club head," because the identical term "swing" is used to designate the player's effort to wield the club, whether it bears any resemblance to a real swing or not. Yet I am convinced that very few players indeed can explain satisfactorily just what is meant by swinging the club head, and further that few high-handicap players really swing in making a stroke.

The above, then, sets forth my conception of the problem involved in teaching others to play. It sounds quite simple, and it is simple – so simple, in fact, that I find it difficult at times to get pupils actually to accept it. For this reason, it becomes necessary to resort to much repetition. If, in reading the text that follows, the reader feels that this is being overdone, I beg him to believe that I have not been able to bring about satisfactory results in any other way, after more than twenty years of seeking.

Good golf is easy to play, and easy golf is enjoyable golf. It is regrettable indeed that so many persons who play golf, or play at it, make such a labor of it. If through the message of instruction presented herein I can help even a small percentage of the great army of laborers at golf to become players, I shall feel highly repaid for my effort.

-Ernest Jones

# −1−

# WHAT IT IS ALL
# ABOUT

Faulty methods of doing a thing obviously add to the difficulties of satisfactory performance. And the difficulty that a great many thousands of people encounter in their efforts to learn to play a creditable and enjoyable game of golf stoutly implies serious faults in the methods they follow in trying to learn the game.

When one has gone along for some time doing a thing in an awkward, cumbersome manner, in order to learn the right way, it becomes necessary first to correct the existing faulty method. Therefore, before setting out to explain my own method of teaching, I want to point out wherein I feel most people make mistakes.

Briefly summed up, I think the fundamental difficulty lies in a negative instead of a positive approach; golfers start from a premise of trying to find out what is wrong when the shot does not come off satisfactorily, instead of getting back to the positive consideration of what it is that causes the shot to prove satisfactory. That this approach is a natural result of the system of teaching employed by their instructors is all the more unfortunate.

I know the old saying that "To know what is wrong is one way of knowing what is right," but I am afraid this is a long and circuitous route to follow in learning to play golf. There are too many wrong ways, when it comes to the matter of identifying these in detail, and the process of elimination in finding eventually what is right proves tedious and discouraging.

This consideration of details of wrong methods suggests the second fundamental difficulty in the approach to learning the game, namely, that of trying to take the stroke apart and identify it piece by piece through visual observation of what this or that good player appears to do as he plays a stroke. This means trying to learn the game solely through application of the sense of sight, whereas every good golfer in the world plays the game through the guidance of the sense of touch or feel.

I know any number of persons who can give you an excellent word picture of what actually takes place as a good player makes a stroke, but who are totally incapable of making a correct stroke themselves. They have watched others, read articles analyzing their actions, and studied pictures of them in various stages of the stroke, until they have an accurate and correct picture of what the action should be, but they are quite incapable of producing the action. Granted that they have chosen excellent models, the basic mistake they make is the failure to realize that, whereas they are watching an expert perform, they are missing entirely the methods employed by the expert in reaching the estate of expertness.

This is quite illogical, because the expert never became expert by following a procedure of this kind. The skillful performer in any line made his start by acquiring a sense of the fundamentals involved. Consciously or subconsciously he acquired mastery of these fundamentals in their proper application, and gradually molded them into his own particular style of performance. It is for this reason that I insist the simplest way to learn golf is to get back to acquiring first an understanding of what it is the good player does consistently that the poor one does only occasionally, if at all.

Briefly stated, every good golfer displays *control, balance*, and *timing* in wielding the club. Without these factors no one becomes a consistently good player. Practically all discussions of the game from the instructive side abound in references to these three points, but usually, when one presses for explicit, detailed explanation of just what is meant by any one or all, the answers received are vague and indefinite.

One hears, for instance, that this or that expert player has fine control. But just what is control, how is it achieved, and what does it mean? In brief, what are we trying to achieve in swinging a golf club? Now, questions on fundamentals of any subject frequently sound simple – so simple, in fact, as to appear ridiculous. The above question may strike the reader as just that. We are trying to strike the ball with the club head, of course. That's obvious, to be sure – so obvious that a great army of golfers, trying desperately to remember half a dozen things, or more, at the time of wielding the club, entirely forget the main purpose.

We are trying to strike the ball with the club head, so it should be plain that we must have control of the club head. Next, what are the dominant factors in the action of the club head in striking the ball? The answer to that is *speed* and *accuracy*. To get maximum distance from the effort, the club head must be traveling at the maximum speed at the instant of impact. So, also, the higher the speed, the finer the degree of accuracy in the well-made stroke, as I shall explain later on. We want maximum speed, and we want it at the right time and place – the instant of impact.

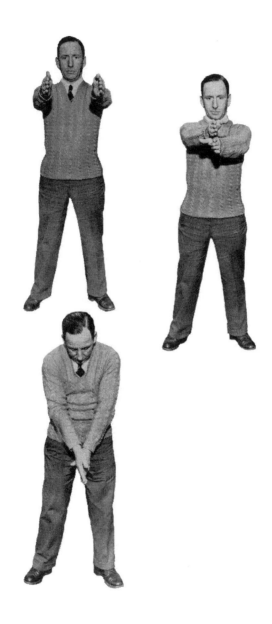

*The first four pictures, show a simple routine for arriving at a position of balance and freedom. First, stand comfortably erect and extend the arms at full length, with the palms of the hands facing; next, bring the hands together, with the right immediately above and touching the left; then lower the hands into position on a vertical center line in front of the body; finally close the fingers as in holding the club. Easy body balance and balance between the two hands result. The fifth picture is introduced to show one position in which this balance has purposely been destroyed by deliberate effort with the hips.*

In approaching the factor of speed and how to attain it, let me first direct your attention to the action of a pendulum. On first consideration, the easy rhythmic movement of a pendulum, on an old-fashioned clock, let us say, back and forth, hardly suggests speed. But reflect a moment; if the arc through which the pendulum is swung is gradually increased, the pendulum must in time move through a complete circle. To move an object in a circular path, the power must be applied at the center. That is centrifugal application of power. It is one of two basic methods of applying power; the other is leverage. In wielding a golf club, one swings the club head with the hands around the center. Centrifugal application of power can and does develop the greatest speed possible from a given supply of power.

Now suppose we look at the movement of the club head in a golf stroke by comparison with the action of a pendulum. It does not matter how long or how short the stroke is; this is merely a matter of the size of the angle through which the pendulum or the club head is moved. No matter how large or how small this angle may be, the nature of the action remains the same and the movement of the club head is always under control. The speed of the movement is dependent on the amount of power applied, but the nature of the response is always uniform.

A swinging action in moving the club head is the source of control in a golf stroke, and it is the only reliable and dependable source. Therefore we arrive at the conclusion that, in order to acquire control, we must learn to move the club head with a swinging action. This must be the chief aim, first, last, and all the time, if we are to acquire a positive and recognizable base on which to build in developing skill in playing golf. It is the one essential present in the stroke of every good golfer. A swinging action dominates the stroke of the experts, one and all, regardless of how different individuals

*Moving a weight back and forth on the end of a string, in this fashion, is possibly the simplest demonstration of a swinging action. A pocketknife attached to the corner of a handkerchief serves the same purpose. Since the handkerchief is flexible, it cannot transmit power through leverage.*

may seem to vary one from another in outward appearance while
playing a stroke.

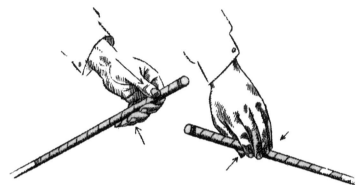

*It is possible to move the head of a golf club in a circular
path, through the application of leverage, as this drawing shows.
Very many golfers have gone on doing so for years, without
learning what is meant by swinging the clubhead.*

The problem of how to acquire and apply control calls for
much fuller discussion, to be taken up in later chapters. I want now to
turn to a consideration of *balance*, second of the three basic factors.
Balance is a state, a condition. It is simple and easily understood.
When a person stands erect with his weight evenly distributed on his
two feet, he displays a simple form of easy balance in condition of
rest or absence of movement. When he walks, he exhibits balance in
motion. In either case he is a ready and simple exhibit of easy balance,
maintained entirely without conscious thought or effort.

Balance in playing a golf stroke starts with a condition of
rest, and develops into a condition of movement. In both phases it is
quite as simple as in standing or walking, if we only cease to look at it
as an end consciously to be attained. Only when we insist on
considering it in the light of transfer of weight, as a matter for

*But here is what happens when pressure or leverage is used in trying to cause the knife on the end of the handkerchief to move back and forth. The flexible medium cannot apply leverage.*

conscious effort, does balance become a perplexing and annoying problem. Obviously, then, we are dragging in unnecessary grief when we insist on thinking out a plan for keeping balanced as the club is moved first back, then forward. The simplest solution to such a problem is merely to put away any thought of trying consciously to maintain balance.

In swinging a golf club through any considerable arc, the body plainly must do a certain amount of turning. That changing of body posture destroys the condition of balance at rest, unless there is a compensating movement to maintain it. That identical situation is true in walking, yet no conscious thought is given to maintaining balance as you walk along under normal conditions over a fairly level or flat surface. When you walk uphill, you instinctively lean forward. You are maintaining your sense of balance in doing so, but you are quite unconscious of a definite purpose in doing so.

This is exactly what should take place in playing a golf stroke. All movement to maintain the condition of balance should be purely responsive to the main purpose of the action you are consciously trying to execute, that is wielding the golf club. In no case should there be a conscious action aimed at maintaining balance as an end in itself. You cannot possibly achieve the two actions at the same time through conscious effort.

The main purpose in playing a golf stroke is to strike the ball with the club head. The hands hold and control the club. You try consciously to control this action through the use and movement of the hands. Maintaining the condition of balance must be responsive to what you are trying to do with your hands, just as it is when you swing a pair of Indian clubs, for example, or perform any of the innumerable other physical acts common in everyday life. You cannot hope consciously to control what you are doing with the hands and at the same time to direct body contortions in an effort to maintain balance. You strike the ball with the club head and you control the club head through the manipulation of the hands, not through the conscious turning or twisting of the body. Forget the latter, and let it respond naturally to the main purpose, as it does in walking.

Coming now to *timing*, suppose we submit the simple question: Just what are you timing? Why , the striking the ball with the club head. Unless you can feel what you are doing with the club head, you cannot possible have any idea or sense of timing. Expressed in one way, timing means producing the maximum speed with the club head at the instant of impact against the ball. From the standpoint of those who prefer to approach the problem of learning golf from the analytical angle of identifying the outward appearance of a correct stroke, timing might be defined as the proper coordination of body, arms, and hands to produce this maximum speed at the designated time. But I doubt that this is going to be very helpful to anybody in learning to develop timing in his own stroke.

Perfect timing is the identification of a true swinging action. It is the essence of rhythm, or measured motion. If you swing a weight on the end of a string, the speed at which the weight can be made to move is proportional to the amount of force applied. Regardless of the speed at which the weight is moved, there is always a feel of the presence of the weight at the end of the string, exerting an outward pull on the source of application, due to the basic nature of centrifugal application. Throughout the movement there is complete coordination or uniformity between the amount of force applied and the result obtained in speed at which the weight is moved. Again, a swinging action is the only positive and reliable insurance for producing and maintaining this uniformity of relation. In other words, a true swing cannot fail to produce perfect timing.

Timing is a product of moving the club head with smooth rhythm. Consider, for instance, the case of a child jumping a rope. Coordination is achieved by centering the attention on the action of swinging the rope with the hands and not on the jumping. The swinging action with the rope lends itself to timing and rhythm, and the act of jumping is attuned to the swinging of the rope. Consider for a moment the difficulty of trying to reverse the procedure.

Let us review what has been said of the three essentials to a correct swing, control, balance, and timing. Control may best and most easily be assured through the use of a swinging action in wielding the club. Furthermore, balance and timing are natural and logical adjuncts of swinging, which result without conscious action or thought on our part; these two factors become troublesome only when we set out to make them objectives of conscious effort.

Control, combining balance and timing, can be attained through developing a swinging action in wielding the club. We sense control through a feeling in the hands of what is being done with the club head. This, I submit, is a positive way to learn golf – to learn what we are doing when we are playing well, instead of worrying about what we are doing when we are playing badly. It affords a definite point of orientation. There can be little satisfaction to a traveler to be told that he is traveling a wrong road to reach an expressed destination, unless he is told also how to find the right road. Learn to swing the club head and to know when you are swinging; this is and for many years has been the basic theme in my teaching.

# —2—

# HOW TO HOLD
# THE CLUB

We strike a golf ball with the head of the club, and we hold the club with the hands. It follows, therefore, that the method of holding the club must be of real importance. The manner of holding any tool or implement must obviously be suited to the way in which it is to be used, if the best results are to be obtained.

It is customary to refer to the manner in which the hands are placed on the club as the "grip." This is, I think, in a measure, unfortunate, because the word "grip" rather implies holding onto something with a viselike tensity. Such tensity is not needed in holding a golf club; furthermore, it will prove a serious obstacle to wielding the club properly. However, since the term is in common usage, it will be used here, but with the reminder that it applies only to the position of the hands as they are placed on the club.

There are three general types of grip, each referring to a specific disposition of the two hands in their relation each to the other. These are the *overlap*, the *interlock*, and the so-call *natural*. In the first, the thumb of the left hand extends diagonally across the shaft, and the pad of the thumb of the right hand rests on it, while the little finger of the right hand is lapped over the forefinger of the left. In the second, the thumb of the left hand extends across the shaft back of the right, while the little finger of the right and the forefinger of the left are interlocked. In the natural grip, the two hands are free from any interlocking or overlapping, the fingers of one hand occupying relatively the same positions on one side of the shaft as those of the other hand do on the reverse side.

Each method has had its exponents among the winners of great championships, although very few players today are to be found using the natural method. I strongly favor and recommend the overlap method for one very important reason, namely, the positions of the thumbs and first fingers of the two hands. These members are of tremendous importance in sensing a feel of the club head, and I consider it necessary that they both have actual contact with the shaft.

Realizing the difficulty of creating word pictures that will leave no doubt of the correct method of placing the hands. I am introducing several photographs and drawings, which show plainly and unmistakably just how the hands are to be placed; thus the rest of this discourse will be devoted to explaining the aim we are trying to attain. In studying the pictures, the reader is asked to keep in mind at all times that the same principle guides one in holding a golf club that applies in the holding of other tools and implements. That is , hold it just securely enough to assure control of it throughout the action.

Let us consider, for example, the holding of a pen for writing. The expert penman holds it just tightly enough to guide it lightly over the surface of the paper. There is no need to clutch it, because the action is not such as to demand it. Gripping a pen quite tightly destroys flexibility and dexterity and merely makes writing difficult. So also with tight gripping in golf. The power for tight gripping is exercised through the back of the hands, and is highly useful in delivering a heavy blow. But in golf the aim is to deliver a swift blow and not a heavy one. There is a distinct difference between the two.

The thumbs and forefingers do not have so much power for gripping but they, particularly the thumb, enjoy a much wider latitude of movement and are, therefore, the leading factors in directing the movement of the club. Also, since speed in wielding the club is a main consideration, it follows that the club is held and wielded largely with the fingers and not with the palm of the hand. For instance, in throwing a stone one holds it chiefly in the fingers, but in laying hold of a rope for a tug or war one holds it in the palms. In golf the club is held in the hand with the fingers. A study of the pictures shows correct position.

In the matter of the relation of the hands, the illustrations show that they are placed so as to face each other squarely. That is to say, if you extend the left arm straight out in front of the body at full length with the palm turned in, then raise the right up to where it just touches the left, also with the palm turned in, and then lower both hands to the approximate position they hold in addressing the ball, you will have the two in the correct positions relative to each other.

This is a "balanced" position, and is entirely logical for the purpose to be served. Thus, if you were to bounce a ball off the floor, the palm of the hand would face straight down; if you were to bounce it against the ceiling, the palm would face squarely upward. In making a golf stroke, the movement is first in one direction and then in the reverse. The hand must, therefore, be placed so as to make movement in each direction equally easy and comfortable.

Reference to the "balance" in hand position, as shown in the pictures, will reveal that the thumb and forefinger on each hand have identical positions on reverse sides of the shaft. This is as it should be to facilitate swinging. Yet I realize that the reader may be ready to point out that he has observed this or that well-known player who departs radically from this position, and he will, of course be quite right in his observation.

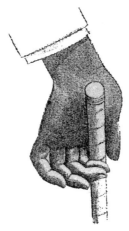 

*The palm side of the left hand showing the correct relation of the thumb to the forefinger.*

*A front view of the thumb and forefinger of the left hand, showing relation of thumb and forefinger.*

But let me say this: I know many fine golfers who play beautiful golf in spite of the handicap of faulty gripping. They happen to have learned that way, and any other method would for the time being feel distinctly awkward if they chose to make a change. At the same time we are aiming at simplifying the game as far as possible, and certainly there is no better place to start than in adopting the right

*Successive steps in placing the hands on the club correctly; upper left, here is the position the shaft occupies in the left hand; upper right, the left has been closed in position here, and the relation of the shaft to the right hand is shown; lower left, just before closing the fingers of the right; lower right, the full application of both hands.*

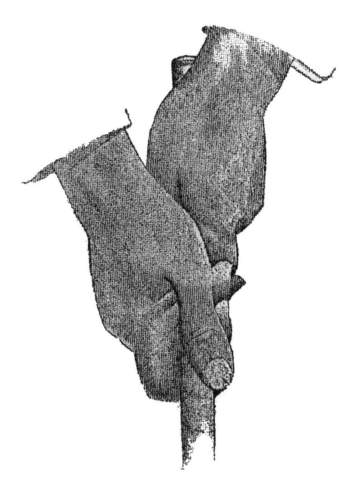

*Correct hand position is important, so that the two hands may work in as full unison as possible. The palms of the two face squarely toward each other, in a balanced position. Both thumbs extend diagonally across the shaft, clasping it between the thumb and forefinger.*

method of holding the club. It will save more than a little grief later on.

Before moving on to consideration of other phases, let me add just a few more words on the amount of tension to be employed in holding the club. It has been my observation that far more high handicap players error through gripping too tightly than through loose gripping; yet laxness in holding the club must be avoided. See that you hold it securely enough to maintain full control throughout.

I have frequently been asked whether or not there should be a loosening of the grip as the club gets to its maximum position in the backswing, in order to allow for ease and freedom in changing the direction in the movement of the club head. Possibly the reader has seen very good golfers do this. But if they did, it was not by design, and in all probability they were not even aware that they did it. A firm, secure hold on the club should be maintained right through the stroke from start to finish.

# —3—

# HOW TO STAND TO THE BALL

Just as the manner in which the hands are placed on the club is of great importance in aiding an easy swinging action, so is the way one stands to the ball important in an easy response on the part of the body to the action of swinging. The position that the feet occupy in relation to each other and also to the location of the ball fixes the foundation on which the action of the stroke is carried out. Plainly, therefore, the character of the foundation will have much to do with the nature of that action.

As in the case of the grip, observation of any considerable number of successful players will reveal quite a range of difference in the matter of stance or the method of placing the feet. By common practice, three general types of stance are recognized – *open, square,* and *closed.* The term in each case refers to the position of the feet as related to the ball and the proposed line of play.

The square stance predominates. It finds the toes of the two feet in a line approximately parallel with the line of play. The open method finds the left foot drawn somewhat back from this line; the stance is called closed when the left foot is advanced nearer the line.

People play good golf using any one of the three. Thirty years or so ago the tendency in England was toward the closed stance. Then along came J.H. Taylor, who stood quite open and won several championships with that method, and straightway it became popular to employ an open stance. In more recent years most of the well-known players came to stand practically square. Within the past few years certain well-known players in this country profess to find particular merit in closing the stance again.

I mention these facts merely to point out that good golf may be played by using any one of the three, and that the simple device of adopting either, because it is strongly advocated or recommended by this player or that, can hardly be relied on to bring about any permanent improvement in a player's game, except in very rare cases. One sees both good and bad golf played with all three types.

It is my feeling that the square method is the most logical and effective, and this is the method that I use and recommend. I do so because I think it provides true balance and also lends itself easily and readily to a free turn of the body in both directions, toward the right on the backswing and toward the left in the downswing. The closed method leaves the body in position for an easy turn in the backswing, but offers restraint in the downswing. The reverse is, of course, true where the stance is open. Players who see fit to depart from the square methods usually do so, after they appear to get better results in their own case, through a process of trial and error in working out adjustments of their swings.

I hope it is evident from the foregoing that the type of stance is not significant; until the player has made enough progress at the game to qualify at adjusting refinements in his play, he will do well to go along with the square position, for there are other things of importance to consider. Fundamentally, the stance should provide a feeling of ease and comfort. The posture should allow the body to yield easily to the action of swinging, with a minimum of tenseness and resistance. As one stands to the ball to begin the business of swinging, there should be a feeling of easy balance. That is to say, the player should feel balanced from side to side and likewise from back to front. It should be just as though he were standing easily erect with the two arms dropped at the sides, in the first preliminary stage. Placing the club head back of the ball will call for his bending forward slightly at the waist, but proper balance will prevent any surging forward on to the toes. The legs should be practically straight at the knees, but with a feeling of easy relaxation in these joints. They should never be stiff or rigid.

Avoid any effort at digging the feet into the ground, as if to engage in a weight-lifting contest or tug of war. Such a procedure sets up a feeling of tenseness in the legs, which will be communicated to other arts of the body; this is distinctly hostile to the easy freedom needed for launching a swinging action. Aim at acquiring the easy freedom that accompanies a simple physical exercise, such, for instance, as one feels on the dance floor just at the instant of picking up the timing of the music to start dancing.

There is no scale of measurement to determine the necessary distance between the two feet, but roughly the width of the stance should be about that of the shoulders. Too wide a stance will restrict the action of the body, while placing the feet too closely together restricts the base of action and tends to disturb balance. Ordinarily the toes should be pointed so as to form an angle of approximately 45 degrees. From time to time one hears of some well-known player who has discovered special merit in standing with the toe pointed

*Front and side views of the square stance, showing, respectively, correct location of the ball in relation to the feet and approximate distance the player should stand from the ball, as indicated by the amount of bend of the body and the distance the hands are extended from the body.*

*Illustrations of closed stance (right) and the open stance (left), the former with the left foot advanced nearer the line of play than the right, the latter with the left foot drawn from the line. The accompanying text explains the variations in both cases.*

slightly inward. This may serve some purpose, but it is not clear to me what it is.

As to the distance one should stand from the ball, clearly the length of the club chosen for the stroke must be a factor. But in any case it is important to bear in mind that the position of the feet is to be determined by first placing the club head in position back of the ball and then adjusting the position, never by taking a position and then adjusting the swing to fit.

It has been suggested above that a slight bend at the waist is necessary to permit the player to take a starting position for the stroke. The prevailing error is toward bending over too much. The body ought to be kept reasonably erect, and, once the position is established, it should be maintained throughout the swing. Straightening up or bending lower cannot but destroy the effectiveness of the stroke.

The keynote to a smoothly timed stroke is a feeling of relaxation* and freedom from tenseness. If there is tenseness either in the hands and arms or in the legs, it will absolutely forestall a swinging action at the start. This prompts me to say a few words about waggling, or the preliminary movement of the club head back and forth over the ball. A few movements of this kind are helpful. They allow the body to relax, and help to provide a feel of the club head. But excessive waggling may become a habit, and an objectionable one. In such a case the practice is probably more harmful than helpful.

The accompanying photographs and drawings will help the reader to identify more readily the correct way to take up a position, and a careful study of them is recommended.

# −4−

# A SWING AND HOW
# TO ACQUIRE IT

Up to this point we have been concerned with pointing out that the basis of good golf is a swinging action, and with describing the methods of holding the club and placing the feet which lend themselves most readily and comfortably to developing and producing such an action. We come now to a consideration of how to acquire that action.

I approach the task with full realization of the difficulties of explaining it in terms that cannot be misunderstood, because it involves describing something that one must feel, and not something that one identifies through sight. It is simple enough to examine an action photograph of any expert player, to point to the position of this or that member of the body, and to explain how these different positions conform with a swinging action. But I have already explained why I think such a practice is of little value in the practical problem of teaching others to play well.

Even at the expense of repetition, then, let me say again that the good golfer has a feel of what he is doing with the club head. He does not see the successive movements that different parts of his anatomy execute through the stroke. Moreover, he never learned to play well through thinking or giving conscious consideration to the working of these different parts, other than to learn how to hold the club properly and how to stand correctly to the ball.

Let me begin by calling attention to the fact that swinging is a definite action in itself, and subject to its own peculiar laws. It is entirely free of, and distinct from, leverage. Swinging and levering are diametrically opposed methods of applying power. In a swing the connecting medium between the power and the object swung has both ends moving always in the same direction; in levering, the two ends of the medium move always in opposite directions. It is no more possible to join up the two in one unified application of power than it is to mix oil and water.

Here again, I think, photographs can be used to advantage to convey the right idea to the reader. I want first to direct your attention to the pictures on pages 40 and 41. I am using here a device familiar to all to whom I have ever given personal instruction, and my constant companion in that kind of work – a pocket knife attached to one corner of a handkerchief, a convenient example of a weight on the end of a string. Examine first pictures 1 and 2. These show the action at opposite extremes, when the knife is swung through approximately half a circle. Observe that the handkerchief is drawn taut, because a swinging action is always an expanding action, with the weight exerting an outward pull.

I would suggest that the reader rig up a similar device of weight and string and try the experiment for himself, guiding the movement entirely through a feel of what is happening with the weight. As long as the weight is being swung, it will keep the string pulled taut, and this condition will prevail whether the swing be short or long.

Examine next pictures 4 and 5. Here I am holding a club along with the handkerchief, executing a swing through approximately half a circle. The handkerchief in its movement serves as a check on whether there is an actual swing of the club head. If I push or pull on the shaft of the club, it may still be moved through a similar arc, but the movement of the knife and the handkerchief will not coincide. Leverage, replacing swinging, may produce a result that appeals to the eye as being quite similar, because the shaft of the golf club is stiff and therefore a suitable medium for levering. But you cannot apply leverage through a highly flexible medium, such as a string or handkerchief.

I should like to emphasize again the fact that feel of the action, and not seeing it, is the necessary essential to its correct understanding, as the above experiments demonstrate. It requires something of an experienced eye to detect at once the difference between a true swinging movement, in moving the head of a golf club through the arc shown in these pictures, and the result that may be attained in a movement brought about through levering. The casual observer may be unable to detect any difference. But the check afforded by moving the club and the string with a weight on the end together is complete and convincing. Furthermore, continued experimentation with this test will finally enable the player to distinguish between the two methods, not only by the sense of sight but by a vastly more important method, so far as learning golf is concerned – that of feeling the difference.

The action demonstrated in these pictures is, of course, that of a pendulum. Its fundamental and distinguishing characteristic is the same whether the pendulum is swung through a small arc or a

*The test of a true swinging movement. First is the movement back and forth of a pocketknife attached to the corner of a handkerchief. Then swinging both a club and the weighted handkerchief together, so that the movement of the two synchronize. Only through a true swing can this be accomplished. Leverage will not cause the weight on the handkerchief to respond in this way.*

large one. The maximum arc is a complete circle, assuming that the power is applied at a fixed center. The golf stroke actually is not a circle, because the center of the stroke, which is the center of gravity of the body, is not fixed throughout the stroke. At the same time the characteristic action of the pendulum is present throughout. No one makes an absolutely perfect swinging action in his golf stroke, but the more nearly he approaches a perfect swing, the steadier and the more consistent the results will be.

"Yes," says one, "all that you have said may be true, and I understand you when you say 'Swing the club head,' but I still do not understand exactly what you mean by 'swinging.' It is clear enough that, when you whirl a weight on the end of a string, you are swinging it, but I don't see just how this kind of swing can be made to coincide with a movement that has to change direction."

Suppose we go back to the pendulum again. One may readily picture a pendulum being swung through an arc of, let us say, 135 degrees, or three-quarters of a half circle. So also with a weight on the end of a string. But possibly it occurs to the objector, from experience of observation, that, if the swing is expanded to 180 degrees or a little beyond, a jerky or uneven action may result just at the instant when the change of direction is effected, although no such condition would develop in the action of whirling a weight through a complete circle.

However, a little reflection will reveal that the same agency which enables the person, swinging a weight on the end of a string through less than half a circle, to expand the arc conveniently to a complete circle without physical hindrance also makes possible the change in direction in the path traveled by the club head, without interference with the characteristic quality of swinging. This agency is flexible wrists, or, more properly, the unified action of the two wrists.

The wrists supply a factor in swinging a golf club that is impossible in a purely mechanical device, for, whereas the arms are in part stiff and rigid, they are also in part flexible. This flexibility in the wrists makes it possible for the golfer both to extend the arc of the swing and to bring about a change in direction without disturbing the rhythmic action characteristic of swinging. A sense of feel of what is being done with the club head takes care of this.

Identifying the correct action of the club head through the sense of touch or feeling is, therefore, the goal for which we are striving. And it is necessary that this feeling be sensed from the very start of action in beginning a stroke. Unless the stroke starts as a swinging action, there is but slight possibility that such action can or will be developed later on. The start is very important, which suggests the thought that probably every golfer at some time or other has found himself pondering over just how the movement should be started.

I have no thought of going into detailed analysis of the movements of different parts of the body in this or any other connection, but I do want to suggest that the answer to this question is quite simple in the light of what has been said about swinging. In producing a swing, the contact at the end of the medium, which transmits the power to whatever is being swung, initiates and guides the action. That is to say, in the case of a right-handed golfer, the left hand is at the end of the shaft, and therefore initiates and directs the movement. The reverse is true with left-handed players.

Understand that golf is neither a right-handed nor left-handed game, but a two-handed one. Otherwise we should play it with either one hand or the other, as we do in tennis for example. But so long as two hands are used, the one at the end of the shaft remains fixed throughout, and therefore is the guiding and direction agency. The same is true, of course, in wielding an ax or swinging a heavy hammer. For a right-handed person, the left retains a secure hold throughout, whereas the right may slide up and down the handle.

In a sense, the shaft of the club is an extension of the left arm, connecting the club head with the left shoulder, or at least forming the line between the two, used in transmitting the power from its source in the body to the club head. The hand, being the extremity of sensitivity in this power line, acquires and transmits the feel of the club head. The sensation, felt in the hands, of what is being done with the club head, is the guide by which conscious effort should be directed. All other physical actions on the part of the body should follow as responsive movement.

So much, then for suggestion on conscious physical effort in starting the stroke. Mental preparation for the start is just as important, possibly even more so. Chief concern here lies in the problem of physical tenseness, brought about by the mental condition that the player is experiencing at the time. Tenseness is an insurmountable barrier to swinging, because swinging implies a free, easy rhythm, which can never be achieved in the face of tenseness. To detect tenseness, let me suggest the following simple experiment.

Hold the club between the thumb and first finger of one hand. Swing the head back and forth, gradually increasing the arc as far as this thumb-and-finger hold will permit. There should be no difficulty whatever in recognizing a feel of the swinging movement of the club head. Now, hold the club with both hands, and resume the movement back and forth. So long as you retain a "feel" of the swinging action of the club, you will observe that the body is moving easily to accommodate the action of the hands and arms. You will recognize complete freedom from any tenseness or strain in any part of the body. There will be tension, in the sense that you feel the "pull" outward of the club head, just as you do in whirling a weight on a string. But there will be no tenseness, in the sense that some part of the body is setting up a resistance to a natural physical response by the body in giving to the action of swinging. Developing of such a resistance interrupts and destroys real swinging action.

The two simple experiments which I have suggested that the reader try for himself, that just above and the one where he is asked to hold both a golf club and a weight on the end of a string, are the most effective devices I can offer for helping him to learn to know and to identify a swing by feel; he must learn it in this way to make any lasting progress in leaning to play golf well. The distinction I have drawn between the mechanics of swinging and levering will, I hope, help clarify his understanding of just what is meant by swinging. But he must go further than that. He must learn to know a swing by its feel, and no one can exercise his sense of touch or feel for him.

Were it possible to convey this message of swinging unfailingly through written words, there would be no need for anything further. However, I am not so optimistic as to hope for such a result. In the first place, I know from long practical experience that a great deal of time and patience is needed to get the message over, even when I have the pupil in hand and am, therefore, able to use personal example and demonstration. Since this is not possible in delivering the message in writing, I pass, therefore, to further consideration of the basic idea from somewhat varied points of view.

# —5—

# TIMING AND RHYTHM

Frequently I am confronted with the statement that any one knows you have to swing the clubhead, but that to play good golf, you have to do a lot more than that. As a matter of fact, you do not have to do more than learn to swing the clubhead in order to strike the ball the most forceful and yet the most accurate blow possible with the power at your command.

You can develop the maximum force at your command by developing clubhead speed in swinging to strike the ball, but you cannot force a swing. I suspect that the latter idea is what persons have in mind when they say you have to do more than just swing the clubhead. I have spoken already of timing, and I have also made reference to rhythm. I have shown how we attempt to time the stroke through a feeling of what we are doing with the clubhead in striking the ball. Furthermore I have asserted that, to do this most effectively, it is necessary to *swing* the clubhead. And perfect swinging is perfect rhythm.

USE THE HANDS TO WIELD THE CLUBHEAD AND

TO SENSE CONTROL OF WHAT IS BEING DONE

WITH IT FROM FIRST TO LAST. ACTIONS BY

*As an aid to grasping the theme of swinging the clubhead with the hands, the artist has omitted body ouline in this series of sketches. You control the movement of the clubhead with the hands and*

OTHER BODY MEMBERS ARE RESPONSIVE ONLY

TO THIS CONSCIOUS PURPOSE OF MAINTAINING

CONTROL OF THE CLUB THROUGHOUT THE STROKE.

*you sense control through feel. Body positions at successive stages of the stroke are results of the action of swinging the clubhead, and are not striven for consciously by the player.*

I once heard a golfer who had followed Bobby Jones through a round of eighteen holes say that he could not identify a single thing that this great golfer did in playing a stroke. Every shot, he added, appeared to be so simple and so easy. And I once heard Miss Joyce Wethered, for whom I have a warm admiration, both for her charming personality and for her ability to play golf so beautifully, say that she had learned a great deal from Mr. Jones by observing his timing and rhythm.

These two observations are most interesting. An expert player herself, Miss Wethered knew and could appreciate that what made Mr. Jones's game seem so effortless was the smooth rhythmic way in which he swung the club. The other observer, bent on discovering and identifying this or that single movement or maneuver, to which he might attribute his subject's fine success, entirely overlooked the most essential thing of all – rhythmic smoothness in the stroke.

It is characteristic of centrifugal application of power, that is, swinging, to appear effortless in its performance. There is no appearance of strain, so evident in levering. A giant wheel spun at a rate of 1,000, 2,000 or more revolutions per minute, may still give no hint of the terrific force driving it because this force is applied evenly and smoothly. But if, unfortunately, a flaw in its construction should result in its flying apart under the force, parts of it may be thrown a great distance and great damage may be done. The power driving a perfectly functioning wheel is there all right, but the method of its application does not readily suggest the force, measured by the results obtained. Likewise, in applying human power in swinging a golf club, the smoother and more rhythmic the swing, the less one is likely to suspect the range of the power solely from watching its application. But the results show in what happens to the ball.

Where fine timing and rhythm exist, there is not only little outward show of the real application of power but also an absence of any feeling of taxing physical effort. This, I think, explains the fact that a great army of golfers do such a deal of straining and surging in their efforts to hit the ball. I am convinced that a very large percentage of these have never in their golfing experiences actually felt the sensation of striking the ball with a real swing. Certainly efforts of this kind make hard physical labor of the game, though it should be no more than light exercise.

I had an excellent illustration of this point in my indoor school during the past winter. A very well-known player came in for instruction. I said "Of course, there can't be very much the matter with you; the trouble with you good players is that you are always trying to find out why you hit a shot badly, instead of learning to understand what it is you do when you hit one well."

"Well, to tell the truth," he said, "sometimes when I am playing well it seems so easy it is actually disappointing."

Exactly, and there is the rub. It was disappointing because, to him, the freedom of timing and rhythm were not recognizable. He had an instinctive feeling that something was lacking, yet by his own admission he was getting highly satisfactory results, playing his best game. Inability to sense timing and rhythm in the stroke, and thus establish a guide toward which he could always turn when for any reason his game began to go bad, left him a victim of worry over what was causing him to go wrong. Once you have learned to sense the feel of timing and rhythm embodied in a real swing, you will always have a definite base on which to check.

If the reader happens to be one of the vast army to whom the game has thus far been largely an exhibition of grunting and groaning, may I suggest the possibility that he has at sometime, purely by accident, struck the ball with a real swing without knowing it. Doubtless he has had the experience of purposely trying to play short of a hazard, when he struck the ball more or less lazily and with little conscious effort, only to see it travel considerably further than he expected, and maybe land plump in the hazard.

What happens in such cases is that the club is actually swung. The urge usually present to knock the ball a long way is missing. The club is moved in a more or less leisurely manner, free from the strain of conflicting movement usually set up through a process of leverage. A fuller discussion of the causes of these conflicting movements will be taken up in a later chapter. But I have brought in here brief mention of the matter, by way of emphasizing the great importance of timing and rhythm.

In line with what has been said of these elements in the swing and the importance of learning to sense their presence in the stroke, I want to make it plain that the player should swing the clubhead in a manner to produce them. This is distinct from any idea that the clubhead swings itself. Nothing would be more absurd than this latter. Yet it has come to me that I teach letting the clubhead swing itself. The clubhead must be moved with a swinging action. Through a feel of what he is doing with the clubhead with his hands.

Timing is felt in the motion of the clubhead. Correct timing is most easily and readily attained through a swinging action. A real swing is truly rhythmic in its nature. In striking a ball with a stick, or bat, or whatnot, correct timing is an absolute essential to satisfactory performance. When the ball is stationary, as in golf, and when no quick change of position by the player, to attain a striking position, is needed, a swinging action can be developed to its full advantage in producing both speed and precision in striking. Swing!

# −6−

# OBSTACLES TO
# SWINGING

A sense of rhythm and smoothness seems to be more highly developed in some persons than in others. Since rhythm is a fundamental characteristic of a swinging movement, this offers a plausible explanation of the greater difficulty encountered by some in learning to swing than by others. Also, I am inclined to believe that women as a rule are somewhat quicker at sensing the action with a golf club than men.

Probably this is because, from early childhood, boys are more accustomed to playing outdoor games than girls. Many of these games employ and develop the application of leverage. I have noticed, for instance, that oarsmen, in particular, generally find it difficult to develop a swinging stroke in golf. Their experience in rowing has been that of using leverage. Similar tendencies, though hardly so marked, can frequently be detected in working with cricketers, baseball players, and tennis players.

But regardless of natural aptitude, or a possible heritage from one's experience at other games, there are always certain

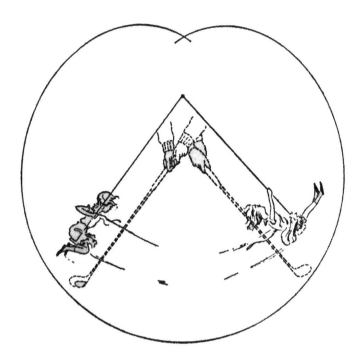

*There is an exact parallel between the action of swinging a golf clubhead with the hands and a child swinging in an old-fashioned swing. In both cases, the start is made slowly with a gradual increase in the application of power to develop speed.*

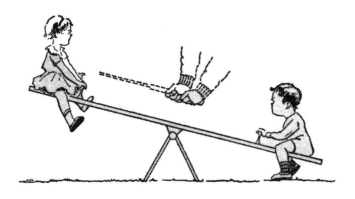

*The "teeter" or seesaw of childhood days exemplifies the principle of leverage, where the two ends of the medium conveying the power move in opposite directions and the characteristic action in applying the power is quick and jerky.*

troublesome factors to be reckoned with. When a golfer steps up to his ball to play a stroke, where distance is a primary consideration, his purpose naturally is to knock it as far as he can. That means to hit it as hard as he can. (Make note of the use of that word "hit".) There is a subconscious urge to use all the power possible. This urge is quite instinctive, but it usually leads to trouble because of the manner in which he tries to apply the power.

The trouble arises from the mental conception he has of hitting the ball. In a sense it is unfortunate that we have become accustomed to the use of the word "hit" in referring to the impact of the club head against the ball, just as I have pointed out earlier that the use of the term "grip" to refer to the manner of holding the club may be misleading. So suppose we take a look at "hitting" in the light of its definition.

The dictionaries define "hitting" as "bringing into violent contact." The synonymous term "striking" is defined as "touching with some force"; also as "giving a blow to." Violence, in a discernible degree, is expressed in "hitting." Violence implies or suggests suddenness, quickness. These are not necessarily implied in "striking." The distinction between the two terms does not involve the amount of force applied so much as it does the manner of its application. It is the manner of the application that is important, representing as it does the difference between swinging and levering, between a sudden, hurried attempt to exert power and a smooth rhythmic one.

There are, to be sure, more ways than one to strike a ball. You can strike it by swinging the clubhead or by employing leverage. You can strike it harder with a swinging action than you can in any other way with the power at your command, and still retain reasonable control over your effort. The principle of centrifugal application of force guarantees this. But it is not likely that you will come to a realization of this of your own accord. To do so is not consistent with your past experiences. Your natural instinct is to try to turn the power on all at once.

A swinging action must begin smoothly and rhythmically, and the force producing it must be applied gradually. There can be no quick jerky movement at any stage of the procedure. As soon as the movement develops this characteristic, the swinging action is destroyed. Steadiness, not speed, is the keynote in beginning the application of the power in a swing. Speed is developed later.

When the player begins the stroke with a mental purpose, however vague, of "hitting," as it has been defined already, subconsciously he tries to make a quick application of the power. As a consequence, he applies it at some intermediate point along the line of communication between the source (that is, the center of gravity of the body) and the other end of the line (that is, the club head). This, as has been pointed out, is quite impossible in an actual swing. It is as though, while swinging a weight on the end of a string with one hand, he attempted to increase the speed of the weight by pressing on the string with the other hand, say halfway between the swinging hand and the weight.

Such a start can result only in a levering action, in which certain parts of the body are set to work at a contrary purpose to other parts, for leverage always finds the two ends of the medium moving in opposite directions. Visible results of this sort of thing are familiar to all of us. One very common form of the malady is to be seen in the chap who pulls his left foot back from its normal position, with nearly all his weight supported on the right leg at the finish of the stroke. An awkward unbalanced position at the finish is positive proof of the use of leverage in wielding the club.

Almost invariably a hurried jerky start in getting the club back travels hand in hand with trouble of this kind. But it is not enough merely to aim at starting the club slowly and deliberately. Such practice may cut down the damage. But a slow start will avail little if the player is contending against conflicting forces. Leverage is leverage, whether it happens to be exemplified by the slow prying of a heavy object with a strong iron bar or by the faster wielding of a golf club.

In like manner, a swing is a swing, whether it be long or short. It always has its own peculiar distinguishing characteristics: the force applied at the center; the object swung always exerting an outward pull; and so on. These characteristics are recognizable by anyone who has learned to identify them through the sense of feel. A player is free to swing just as fast as he can, so long as he knows from the sensation relayed through feel with his hands that he is maintaining a real swinging action with the clubhead.

The foregoing may, I suppose, be called difficulties of natural impulse. They are born of the basic urge to apply all available power for knocking the ball as far as possible, and they are schooled in experience with other applications of physical power. They would be entirely reasonable difficulties in the case of a person who might try to hit a ball with a club the first time he saw one.

But there are other sources of difficulty, deriving from an entirely different background, which prove serious hindrances to thousands of golfers.

I refer now to the obstacles that the player sets up through trying to imitate the style of another, or, I might better say, through imitating certain outward appearances of some player whom he has chosen as a pattern or model. In the first place, the chances are that the observer has chosen for imitation certain actions that are no more than mannerisms at best. They are, in all probability, quite incidental, and of little or no importance. Dozens of these have been picked up, and elaborately explained in so-called instructive treatises on the game as a basic keynote to the skill exhibited by the player in question. I hardly need add that any such contention is pure rot.

Furthermore, if the observer is fortunate enough to identify and interpret correctly the movements of one or more parts of the body essential in swinging the club, he still has little, if any, chance of using his observation to advantage in improving his own play by consciously trying to reproduce the outward physical appearance of it. To do this is to fail to realize that this outward appearance is in reality quite incidental, so far as his model is concerned, to the important business of swinging the clubhead. This is the vital thing in the stroke, regardless of when and how the model acquired it.

Rest assured that the expert has never in any case developed his stroke into a swinging action by giving any conscious thought to the many different details with regard to what the different parts of his anatomy were doing. Remember, too, that the observer is watching the expert perform after the latter has attained the state of expertness. And in all likelihood he is forgetting the important matter of how expertness was attained. If you watch a skillful player perform merely in order to enjoy the artistry he displays, it is enough to dwell on the outward appearance of his style. But if you are trying to improve your own game, go back to the formula by which he developed his artistry.

Watching a great runner in action or a clever dancer rarely suggests his infancy, when he was learning to walk. Yet as a baby this expert had to lay the foundation for his later superb skill by the slow, laborious process of acquiring a feeling of balance in placing one foot before another. That was the groundwork, and without it, of course, there could have been no progress toward his becoming an expert in his particular line.

No golfer should concern himself with trying consciously to copy the playing form of another, once he has reached an age when his inclination is to analyze action in terms of different movements. Fifty years ago Sir Walter Simpson wrote: "For you or me to model ourselves on a champion is about as profitless as to copy Hamlet in the hope of becoming Shakespeare." That statement was true then, and it is true now. Expert players differ in their swings even as they do in the way they walk. Among all the golfers I have ever seen, I would hesitate to say that I had ever seen any two who swing exactly alike. Yet the basic principles are the same for all in swinging a golf club, even as they are in walking.

"Yet," says one, "I have frequently heard it said that certain young players swing almost exactly like their teachers."

That may be true. I have known a great many players whose style reflected that of older players who had come under their observation while they were learning. But don't accept that fact as a rebuttal to the advice against avoiding any effort to copy consciously the style of another, if you are trying to learn and have reached the age when you are capable of recognizing such a thing as style in swinging the club.

Learning to play golf as a youngster and learning after you have reached mature years are two different matters, for the very simple reason that the child still has the benefit of imitative instinct with which nature endows the young of all animals. But as the capacity to reason things out and to analyze actions begins to develop, the imitative instinct begins to fade. A child watches a performance and his mind registers a picture of the action as a whole. He will be unable to analyze it in detail and to describe its successive stages, but imitative instinct will enable him to make a creditable effort at reproducing the action as a whole after he has watched it a few times.

Along this line a rather interesting story went the rounds some years back concerning Bobby Jones and his first appearance in the United States Amateur Championship, at the age of fourteen. A well-known golf writer, watching him drive from a tee some distance away, is said to have remarked that he could almost believe that it was Stewart Maiden hitting the ball. Maiden was the instructor at the club in Atlanta where the youngster started golf. Also Maiden was a boyhood chum in Scotland of the golf writer, who was quite familiar with his swing. I can't vouch for the truth of the story, but it is a good one just the same. Incidentally, it is told of Mr. Jones that as a small boy he was an excellent mimic, and used to amuse friends of the family with his imitations of the peculiarities of different more or less eccentric players at the club.

It is quite logical that youngsters, boys especially, since they are more likely to take readily to the game, should come to pattern their efforts on the performances of those who come under their observation. It is the instinctive thing, because of their imitative capacity. Furthermore, they will naturally select the better players as models, and players of this class swing. Imitative reproduction therefore takes the form of swinging, and in time the swinging action becomes habitual, quite without conscious effort to make it so, other than as the imitative instinct directs.

However, as has been pointed out, such instinctive imitation is a different process entirely from a conscious attempt to copy this or that detail of the action by a person who has watched a swing and succeeded in picking up only a few highlights, so to speak, through attempting to analyze the action from observation. To appreciate the contrast, recall the remarkably easy rhythm you have observed when a caddie has sneaked a swing with one of your clubs, contrary to the caddie master's instruction, and then think back to the efforts you have seen in players to acquire a finishing pose with the club back over the left shoulder, after going through all kinds of contortions in swiping at the ball.

There is difficulty enough for most of us in learning how to swing by the simple process of coming to sense the action through feeling what is being done with the clubhead, without adding to the problem by trying to imitate the appearance of others at the same time. Your gait in walking may not be so elegant as that of others, but it gets results. We cannot all be fine stylists, but we can all develop form in doing a thing if we go about it in an intelligent way. Form refers here to a capacity to do a thing many times over in substantially the same way. Development of a swinging action is the surest and safest approach to acquiring dependable form in striking a golf ball.

# —7—

# VARIATIONS IN
# THE SWING

I should not be surprised to learn that some are disappointed at the failure, up to this point, to find any specific reference on how to use the different clubs in the bag, such, for instance, as "How to Drive," "How to Play the Mashie," and so on. I know that it is quite customary to go into detail on the discussion of the use of different clubs. So let us clear this matter up here and now. The golf stroke, in its basic essentials, is the same with all clubs.

From the driver or brassie right down to the putter, it is a swing. You may vary the swing, but you must not vary from it. I have already stated that I cannot say I have ever seen two players swing exactly alike. Yet there are thousands of good players, and all of them swing. No further proof is needed of variations in the manner of swinging.

Moreover, all good golfers can and do vary their own swings at times to meet the peculiar requirements of the stroke to be played. If, for example, conditions of play require that the ball be made to rise abruptly on being struck, the player not only chooses a club with plenty of loft but he also executes a notably upright swing. Yet he *swings* the clubhead just the same. The plane in which it is swung changes naturally.

Playing from difficult lies likewise involves special problems in adapting the swing to meet the existing conditions. In dealing with an uphill or downhill lie, for example, the player must make due allowance for maintaining his sense of balance through the stroke. But this in no puzzling problem so long as he has acquired the knack of swinging so that it has become habitual. He has to do the same thing in walking uphill or downhill or along the side of a hill. But he gives no conscious thought to the adjustments necessary to these special conditions. His muscular actions respond to the central purpose of keeping the body balanced, without conscious effort to do so. So also in playing a golf stroke.

There is a popular belief that the stroke with iron clubs is more of a hit than with woods. It may be conceded that, in watching even an expert player, one may sense more of what may be called "punch" with wood clubs. The reader will recall the distinction, between "hitting" and "swinging" made in an earlier chapter. Also I may repeat an earlier assertion that no one swings perfectly. There is always an impulse to use more power than we can apply properly, that is, by swinging. When we inject more power than we can control, we introduce a degree of leverage, but, when it creeps in near the end, that is , just before impact, it may produce no appreciable damage, provided the stroke has started as a swing and this action has been maintained almost up to the instant of impact.

Furthermore, whatever of leverage is introduced in the brief instant just preceding impact is restricted to pure hand and wrist action, and does not involve conflicting actions between body movement and arm movement, which are bound to follow the introduction of leverage in starting the stroke. That is to say, if a levering method of applying the power in wielding the club prevails in starting the stroke, the later cannot develop as a swing. On the other hand, if the action is a swing from its inception, the hands and arms will swing on through, maintaining the swinging characteristic as the dominant movement, even though some small degree of leverage develops through the hands and wrists just before and at impact.

There is another ready explanation of the appearance of more "hitting" or "punch" in the stroke with irons, where the stroke is less than a full swing. For these shorter strokes, obviously the turning of the body both on the backward and on the forward swings is not so full as with a full-length swing. Yet the bending or flexing of the wrists is quite as full. For, if the player swings the club, the weight of the clubhead will pull the hands to where the wrists are fully bent, before the change in direction by the clubhead begins to take place.

Also it should be borne in mind that the wrists act as hinges, so to speak, joining the hands and arms, and that the natural outward pull of the clubhead is built up to a maximum at impact, in a real swinging action, quite independent of a conscious attempt to put "wrist snap" into the stroke. It is obvious, of course, that the action of the wrists at the stage where the clubhead is changing direction brings about a position of the hands, in their relation to the forearms, quite different from that in the address. It is equally obvious that the hands must come back to a like position in the address, so that the face of the club shall be brought squarely against the ball. But this return to position can and will be brought about by a swinging action, without conscious effort on the player's part to put so-called "wrist snap" into the stroke.

*Leo Diegel, well-known professional,*
*has scored in the low 70's for a round, playing each stroke, while*
*standing on his right foot alone. This sequence of pictures shows*
*him at varying stages in the swing, and is offerd here as proof that*

*balance during the swing is responsive to the
main purpose of swinging the clubhead with the hands. Diegel
gives no thought to the details of how the body turns, whether
playing from one foot or two.*

On the other hand, conscious efforts on the part of the player to gain distance by striving to introduce wrist action almost invariably lead to trouble. For the expert player, it usually means a shot far off the intended line, more often than not to the left. In his effort to get extra distance, he introduces leverage through too powerful action with the right hand. Remember that, since the left hand is the one on the end of the club, it must guide and direct the action. If the right is allowed to inject too much power, the extra power takes the form of levering.

For the high-handicap player, conscious efforts to introduce wrist action also result in levering. The chief reason for his being a high-handicap player is his failure to learn a swinging action with the clubhead in the first place, but the result he gets will probably differ from that of the more expert player in that his effort at "putting the wrists into it" finds the forward sweep of the hands practically stopped by the time the clubhead reaches the ball, except for a kind of forward flick of the wrists. This, I repeat, is what usually happens when the high-handicap player purposely tries to introduce wrist action consciously.

The foregoing paragraph does not mean to imply that the wrists do not perform an important function in swinging the club. They are vastly important. As I have explained, they make it possible to retain the easy smooth rhythm of a swinging action through the change in direction of the clubhead from the preliminary back sweep of the clubhead until it has been swung up and around at the finish of the swing. But their action, like that of other parts of the body, should be entirely responsive to the main purpose of causing the clubhead to move with a swinging action.

Thus, if it has appeared to you that the stroke with an iron club is more of a hit than that with a driver or brassie, be assured that

*Playing a stroke from a sitting position, a demonstration used to show that no concern need be felt for whether the legs, hips, or other parts of the body will do their respective parts, so long as the player is conscious of swinging the clubhead with his hands. The actions of these members during the stroke are responsive, not initiative.*

the same guide to controlled speed in the full stroke, that is, a swing with the clubhead, is just as important with the irons. Be content with developing that sense of feel of what is happening with the clubhead for irons as well as for woods.

Of course, one varies the swing from long strokes to short ones, in the sense that the action is cut down. But again there is no variation in the character of the action; it is still a swing from the tee shot right down to the putt. Strangely enough, there appears to be more difficulty in maintaining the swing in the shorter strokes, until one has thoroughly developed the idea of sensing a feel of the clubhead at all times, than in the longer ones. Even among very good players one usually finds more badly played short strokes than full ones.

A probable reason for this is that the longer action of the full strokes afford more time to acquire a feel of the clubhead. With the short ones there is a tendency to hurry the thing through and have it done with. Always a hurried stroke is more likely to be marked by leverage. And a hurried start has no place in a swing, which always begins slowly and smoothly.

In this connection, I want to say a word for the benefit of those who are inclined to feel that they must strike a certain kind of pose in order to bring about a stroke which they assume resembles that of some player they have seen. Invariably they assume a position for starting the swing, which is supposed to develop a certain position at the top of the backswing or at some other stage of the stroke. Needless to say, they are thinking in terms of body posture and not in terms of hand action.

One can swing a club from almost any position, if one understands what swinging means and knows how to identify it through feel. The reader has possibly at some time or other watched trick-shot performers hit the ball from different awkward stances and positions. I can sit in a chair and drive a ball 200 yards, and I frequently use this simple device to prove to pupils that, whereas there is one simple and comfortable way to stand to the ball, as has already been described, there are many ways that one may stand and still swing. The important thing is to learn to swing, and to know when you are swinging and when you are not. You will develop your own pattern of swinging just as you have developed that of walking, and you may vary it from time to time consciously, or even sub-consciously. In fact, your will be a rare exception if you are ever able to swing in exactly the same way day after day for any given length of time. But the ability to swing and to know a swinging action by feel is the only hope for permanent improvement in golf.

# −8−

# ACCURACY AND HOW
# IT IS ATTAINED

In an earlier chapter I asserted that both greater speed and greater accuracy in wielding the clubhead can be attained, with a given amount of force, through a swinging application than in any other way. Considerable space has been devoted to the factor of speed. Now I want to take up the matter of accuracy in bringing the face of the clubhead against the ball at the desired angle.

For purposes of comparison, consider the action of a spinning top. It is the rotary motion in a horizontal plane that causes the top to stand on end, in defiance of the pull of gravity, so long as that rotary force is strong enough to resist the pull, which eventually causes the top to fall on its side. The faster the top spins, the steadier the orbit in which it turns. It is only when the spinning speed begins to slow down perceptibly that the top begins to wobble, and eventually falls.

The characteristics of a swing action are the same in all cases, no matter how the action is manifested. Hence the greater the speed developed in swinging the clubhead, the steadier and truer the orbit in which it is swung. But regardless of the speed, a swinging action is necessary to keep the clubhead moving in substantially the same path time after time. In other words, only the steady, smooth application of power exemplified in a true swing will enable the player to approach consistency in wielding the club with accuracy.

Only scant consideration is needed to convince one of the improbability that any player, with the hands placed at one end of a club and the clubhead at the other, from 36 to 40 inches apart, can consciously direct the forward movement of the clubhead so as to strike the ball with the accuracy needed to hit it along the intended line. A variation of 1 degree would mean something like 10 feet in 200 yards, and 3,4, or 5 degrees would be a small margin of error in trying consciously to regulate the angle of striking. It should be plain, therefore, that there can be little hope for accuracy along this line.

Accuracy and control are not to be obtained in this manner in golf any more than a baseball pitcher acquires control in throwing the ball where he wants it to go by thinking of such details as the exact instant at which he releases his hold on it. The pitcher develops control by developing a muscular routine, through constant practice, until he reaches a stage where he instinctively releases his grip on the ball without any conscious thought whatever of that detail. Once he has attained this stage, he will, as a rule, be able to throw the ball accurately so long as he employs the speed that his muscular routine normally develops. But when he tries too hard to develop extra speed, he will probably find difficulty in maintaining control.

The situation is quite the same with the golfer. Once he has developed a muscular routine founded on swinging, he can go on time after time wielding the club with accuracy, and at the same time developing as high a speed as the power employed is capable of producing. But so long as he plays golf, so long will the impulse to apply more power than he can control seize him from time to time. He may exert a more powerful physical effort, but it is likely that the extra power will be misapplied. That is, it will not radiate from the center. As must always be the case in a real swing, but will be introduced in the form of leverage, through application at some other point.

When the baseball pitcher begins to have difficulty in controlling the pitch, he does not try to regain his control by tampering with his method of holding the ball or by trying to throw harder. On the other hand, he attempts to get back to his normal movement in throwing. He knows full well that he has a better chance of bringing the pitch under control in this way than by any other. Once more the case is the same with the golfer.

The only safe and reliable way to get back to striking the ball squarely with the face of the club is to make sure of three things: first, see that the club is being held correctly; second, see that you are standing properly in relation to the ball to hit it where you are aiming; third, make a smooth free swing. If the player holds the club properly, stands in the correct position, and takes a normal swing, the ball must travel in the line selected, or very close to it. These are the three considerations that determine control of direction. Failure to obtain it in a shot can be traced back to the lack of one or more of them in playing the stroke.

I would like the reader to ponder the preceding paragraph carefully. It is very important, especially in consideration of the claim that "one must do more than swing the clubhead" to play good golf. This assertion, I take it, is prompted by observation of the difference in outward appearances of well-known players, and again is evidence that the observer is concerning himself with nonessentials and is missing entirely the basic fundamental – that all good players swing.

*Further demonstrations of precision and timing through swinging. Note coincidence of the club shaft and the weighted handkerchief at the bottom; also exact coincidence between the two, swung singly in the two hands above, the weight pulling the handkerchief perpendicularly upward.*

The point of confusion is that the observer watches certain detailed movements and actions, which he takes to be essential to the player's success. If he followed carefully any player of his choice, he would observe that these mannerisms are present with the player when he is playing below his best form, even as they are when he is playing especially well. But that point is likely to escape him. He also would, if he questioned his model, get the answer that, when the latter is playing well, he is playing very easily; furthermore that, when he begins to play badly, the harder he tries, the more difficult the game becomes.

Whether his model has analyzed his own game well enough to know it or not, it is smooth, easy stroking with a correct grip and stance, which produce for him satisfactory distance, and fine control of direction as well. It distinctly is not some pet device that he is trying out at the time, to enable him to produce consciously accurate control or greater distance, except as such a device prompts him to swing more smoothly and steadily.

It is quite easy to understand the deduction of those who study the playing of the game from the viewpoint of outward appearances, in arriving at the conclusion that certain mannerisms are of importance. It is equally easy to understand the derivation of differences in mannerisms. Reference now is to those who play well, of course. That they do play well is evidence that the stroke with them is basically a swing. How they came to attain it is immaterial. But each is an individual, and, if he has attained mature age, he has without doubt done no little experimenting. He has resorted to the old practice of trial and error until he has worked out something that he is convinced is best suited to his own needs.

Experiments of this kind may run through considerable range, in change of grip, stance, body adjustment before starting the swing, waggling, and so on, until the player eventually works out at least a temporary solution of his problem. Actually, the change may involve to a mild degree a physical handicap, but, if it happens to produce results temporarily, it may afford a real help on the mental or psychological side. The player sets his mind at ease in the conviction that his new discovery is going to solve a certain problem. This done, he is then much more likely to swing smoothly and steadily.

I know a case of a well-known businessman, who consistently cuts seven or eight strokes off his score when playing with a certain noted professional by employing a very simple procedure. For each stroke, the professional takes his stance to play the stroke, marks his footprints distinctly, and then tells his companion to stand in those tracks and hit the ball. This man has been playing golf for years, and it would be utterly ridiculous to suppose that he does not know how to stand to the ball to play a stroke. But the simple trick of having the professional indicate the exact stance removes from the other man's mind all doubt as to whether he is standing properly, and helps him to concentrate on making the stroke.

I have mentioned this case for the simple purpose of showing how the mental aspect of the game affects the physical, a subject that will be taken up more fully in the following chapter, and also for the purpose of tying up with the discussion of accuracy through swinging the many various devices that are supposed to come under the heading of other things that one may be called on to do, besides swinging the clubhead. As stated above, it is not an uncommon thing to find players employing certain devices that actually make the game harder for them. I am referring now to good players. Faulty gripping, exaggerated types of stance, and so on are included in such a list.

Such players play well, and might play even better, and certainly more consistently, with sounder methods. Yet their scoring is such as to bring them to the attention of others who are trying to improve their play. They have acquired the basic fundamental of swinging, and many of their mannerisms, as stated above, may actually make swinging more difficult than it should be. Such physical handicaps in handling the club must in time take their toll. This fact accounts for the great amount of experimenting that goes on even among good players. Among so-called "duffers" this sort of thing is vastly multiplied. There are and have been numberless "tips" supposed to cure this fault or that. Naturally enough, some of them are entirely sound and consistent with correct stroking of the ball. But even these have the shortcoming of dealing only with some single phase of the stroke, whereas the latter is a unit action that cannot be taken apart and treated piece by piece. Other tips and suggestions are far worse because they are not even consistent with correct stroking.

But the worst feature of this approach to learning the game is the fact that it means going about the task backward from the very first. It is a matter of correcting that which is wrong, instead of learning that which is right. A tip to correct one fault may in time produce an equally damaging fault of itself. Furthermore, no matter how much of this sort of thing is done, the fact remains that any plan which supposes that the player is bringing about control in any way other than by smooth swinging from a sound base is doomed to failure.

One of the leading golf writers in this country once remarked: "Bobby Jones trusts his swing to a higher degree than any other golfer I have ever seen. If he is off line on a shot, he may be off 30 yards. Some of the other stars appear to sense that something is wrong, and to make at least a partial correction in the hand action as the clubhead is brought against the ball. But once Jones starts his swing, he goes right through with it without any attempt at correction."

This is nothing more than saying that Mr. Jones was more intent on swinging the clubhead than the others. And over a period of ten or eleven years during which he played in Open Championships, it may be recalled that he was far and away the most consistent player of them all. This remarkable consistency – in the eleven United States Open Championships in which he took part he never once scored as high as 80 – is eloquent testimonial to his success at achieving accuracy in striking the ball through "trusting his swing," as compared to the efforts of others who may have tried to introduce corrective measures through conscious manipulation in the course of making the stroke.

Such efforts to control the club by conscious direction are usually referred to as "steering," and the consequences are well known to all experienced players. They are the result of conscious interference with the performance of an action which normally is, and in all cases should be, subconsciously controlled. This is manifested in the results obtained when one tries to play a stroke with restraint quite as much as when one tries to overdo it. Both cases involve the same difficulty – conscious interference. The results emphasize the necessity of depending for accuracy as well as for speed of the clubhead on developing a swinging action, which is sensed and controlled through feeling in the hands what is being done with the clubhead.

# —9—

# THE MENTAL SIDE

Any general discussion of golf and how to play it well must take note of the mental side of the game. One frequently hears it said that golf is largely a mental problem, and in one respect that is undoubtedly true. It all depends on what is to be considered the "mental side" of the game. If reference is to the conscious thought required in wielding the club, this is of little consequence. No considerable amount of intelligence is needed to swing a club.

On the other hand, if reference is to one's mental activities in the course of playing a stroke, and the complications these may introduce, the "mental side" is indeed of very great importance, because one's mental processes, conscious and subconscious, direct one's physical actions, and it is a dominant characteristic of the conscious processes that they interfere with the subconscious processes. In golf they affect high and low alike, because they interfere not only with the proper performance, after it has been developed to a stage where it can be taken care of subconsciously, but to the learning of the performance in the first stages.

It should be apparent to any player, on brief reflection, that he plays golf, if he plays it well, largely through subconscious control, even as he does a thousand other commonplace things every day of his life. Through one process or another he develops a muscular routine, which from constant repetition becomes habitual, that is to say, subconsciously controlled. Once this has been accomplished, he goes along repeating the performance whenever a situation demands it, without any conscious consideration of the manner in which it is done.

Consider, for example, the simple process of signing one's name. The reader surely could write his signature a thousand times, and each and every specimen would be readily recognizable as being essentially the same as every other. Moreover, he could do so while sitting and chatting with an acquaintance or otherwise employing his conscious mental processes. But make the following simple test: Write your signature as you ordinarily do. Then, in the space beneath it, try consciously to copy it, directing each successive move of the pen or pencil to produce each letter in exact likeness of the one above. Then compare the two, and consider the difference.

It may also be observed that the easier, smoother, and more flowing the natural action of the pen in the ordinary manner of writing, the more pronounced will be the difference. There is distinct rhythm in a free, easy style of writing; in fact, rhythm is highly essential to good penmanship. And rhythm, of course, is also essential to a proper stroking of the ball in golf. There is an exact parallel between the two performances as regards direction by subconscious control and direction by conscious control.

The urge, intentional or otherwise, to try to control the movement of the clubhead through consciously directed effort interferes with the golfer, whether he is a beginner or an expert. In the case of the latter, it explains his lapses from form from time to time. In the case of the former, it explains most of the troubles he has in learning to develop the routine of correct stroking, which is the foundation of any permanent improvement in his play.

*Efforts during the swing to concern the conscious mind with any one of numberless details of the outward appearance of someone else must inevitably interfere with subconscious control of the swing. You should think only of sensing a feel of what you are doing with the clubhead through the action of the hands.*

In the case of the expert, it is said that he is unable to concentrate properly, which prompts me to remark that concentration is probably the most misunderstood term in golf. It does not mean actively thinking of any one detail of the stroke, but rather the opposite – refusal to allow any single detail to absorb the attention. Frequently, when a player thinks he is concentrating very hard on the stroke he is about to play, he is doing nothing more than worrying over one detail of the stroke, or possibly, what is even worse, over the probable outcome of the stroke; sometimes he is worrying to such an extent that he permits his muscular system to tighten up to a point where it is a physical impossibility for him to effect a real swing.

However, the purpose here is to serve first those who are still laboring with the problem of laying the foundation for a consistently good game, that is, those who have as yet to learn how to swing and how to know when they are swinging. So it is the main job to get ahead with the discussion of the mental problems that beset them in this important task of learning to swing.

Too much imagination is a serious stumbling block to most persons in learning to play golf. Imagination is an active function of conscious thinking. It is one of the most important factors in the lives of all of us. We begin exercising it in childhood, and go right along through life indulging it every day. Yet, when it comes to learning to play golf, what a wonderful thing it would be to be able to turn off the imagination just as we do at a faucet. That, of course, is quite impossible, for the imagination will continue to function during our waking hours, whether we wish it or not, and the field of golf is no exception in its range of activities.

I have given lessons to thousands of golfers, and nine out of ten of them were quite willing in the beginning to tell me what was wrong with their games. Actually, of course, if they had known, they should not have felt any need to come to me, or to go to anyone else for instruction. But they overlook this inconsistency in the enthusiasm of their theorizing about the game. Within a short time after a person has taken up golf, almost form the beginning, he begins to form certain conceptions of the stroke and how it is made. Invariably these conceptions take form from what he has been able to gain through the sense of visual observation. On the basis of these observations, his imagination goes to work in formulating different theories.

You may recall from the Foreward a quotation from Sir Walter Simpson, written fifty years ago, on this matter of theorizing. As he pointed out, we have to stand for theorizing on the player's part as a concession to him as a thinking animal. But he must recognize it as a recreation and understand that it may easily prove one of the most serious obstacles to his progress in learning to play well.

Already I have called attention to the necessity of learning the game through the sense of touch or feeling, not through the sense of sight. This fundamental fact explains a great many of the golfer's difficulties, which arise from his theorizing. He is making the serious mistake of trying to reproduce certain physical actions that he has seen in others. It is beside the point that these actions are entirely orthodox and consistent with fine stroking. The matter of chief concern is to develop the method of stroking, and the model himself never developed his method in that way.

Let me illustrate how easily such a mistake can interfere with the orderly and positive way of learning through cultivating a sense of feel of the correct action. A short time ago, I had a pupil who had been making very satisfactory progress through several lessons. In the course of talking things over one day, I emphasized the necessity of starting everything together in beginning the swing, as contrasted with making this or that movement the initial one. In explaining this point further, I remarked that the hands must swing the club back, and that it must not be pushed, pulled, or hauled. While I was demonstrating just what I meant, the pupil noticed that my hands appeared to start slightly before the clubhead was moved.

Nothing was said of this matter at the time, but the action made an impression on his mind, and, in the light of what I had said, he concluded that this was wrong and something to be avoided. When he came back a few days later for another lesson, I noticed right away that something had halted his progress. Tenseness and stiffness were readily evident in each of his attempts to swing the club. I asked him what had caused him to tighten up, and he then told me what he had observed about the movement of the hands during the demonstration in the previous lesson. He had been watching his hands during practice swinging in the meantime and had been trying to keep them from moving as mine had.

Now, as a matter of fact, that particular action of itself was of no consequence whatever. There are many fine golfers who appear to "drag" the clubhead back from the ball. It is quite possible that some of them may have adopted the practice by design, because they were convinced that it served a certain purpose, such, for instance, as insuring freedom and flexibility in the wrists, or guarding against holding the club too tightly. But here again we are considering nothing more than mannerism, and neither this nor any other such small device ever made anyone a good golfer. Undoubtedly such a player had already learned the knack of swinging, and this "drag" was incidental. More than likely, should it occur to the player that he might achieve better results by starting hands and clubhead together, he could, with but little practice, entirely eliminate this little business.

Yet even so small a thing as that proved a definite interruption to that particular pupil. He could not restrain his imagination from attaching importance to the relation of what I had said to him about pushing, pulling, or hauling the club back to the fact that he observed my hands describe a certain movement while I was demonstrating faulty ways of starting. The imagination is constantly operating with information and intelligence communicated to the mind, and it so happens that the sense of sight is the most important of all the senses in gathering such information and intelligence. His sense of sight could detect the physical appearance of the action, whereas his sense of touch could not, of course, register the feel that I, who was wielding the club, experienced.

Then again, I find that most persons appear to retain certain mental reservations in the face of any statement of fact made to them, without necessarily implying any distrust of the source of the statement or of the actual authenticity of the facts. All of us incline toward the feeling that somehow or other we are the exceptions to the general rule.

I fully appreciate the possibility that the reader, at this very instant, is experiencing reservations to statements set forth here and earlier in these pages. Possibly he questions the fact that greater speed and greater accuracy in striking the ball can be developed, with any given amount of power, through swinging than otherwise. He may not be entirely convinced that a more dependable routine of stroking can be developed by learning to sense a swinging action with the clubhead than by any other process. Well, I have conceded that it is possible for persons to learn to play golf through a process of visual analysis of the stroke, as made by others. Through its varying phases, in time piecing these several detailed movements together, but I insist that this is the difficult way. In support of my claim, I can point to countless thousands who have been trying to do this for many years with no appreciable success.

I have touched on these matters, bearing on the difficulties that the imagination or conscious mental processes may and do introduce into the problem of learning to play golf. Much more might be said as to how the mental state affects the player during the playing of a stroke. In the discussion of Obstacles to Swinging, reference was made to how the mental attitude of the player can and does prompt him to try to inject more power than he can control, and, by so doing, causes endless difficulties through converting the application of power from a swing to levering. There are additional difficulties arising from the player's concern over the probable outcome of the shot at hand.

He may, for example, be concerned with danger from a near-by boundary line, which may take its toll of a crooked shot, or a hazard to be carried, or the selection of the proper club, and so on. All these come, of course, under the heading, the mental side. They are all to be treated with the same prescription. Learn to settle the issue in advance of the start of the stroke, and, once that has been started, concentrate only on the idea of feeling the swinging action of the clubhead.

Obviously we cannot will the mind to remain absolutely blank. It must concern itself with something, and there may be a thousand things more or less that will engage its attention, unless we can discipline it to concern itself with some one definite thing. Aim at making that one thing consciousness of a feel of swinging the clubhead. Try to think of that and nothing else.

In this connection, I may recall to the reader's attention what has been said about the sense of sight, and the importance it has in conveying impressions to the mind. Just as it reveals more than any of the other senses, so it is the medium of introducing more interferences and distractions, when one tries to concentrate on any one thought. Therefore, in practicing to learn to sense a feel of swinging the clubhead, it is helpful to close the eyes while swinging. You will note at once that the sense of touch or feel functions more readily when the sense of sight has been shut off. This suggestion has proved very helpful with a great many of my pupils in actual teaching.

# –10–

# PROFIT FROM
# PRACTICE

In a sense, what has gone before has been presented with a twofold purpose. First, I have tried to point out that one must accept the golf stroke as a swinging action of the clubhead, in its basic essential, in order to make any permanent headway in learning to play the game consistently well. The second phase has been an outlining of ways and means of developing a swinging action in wielding the club, through learning to know it and to identify it by the feel as experienced in the hands.

Once this has been done, the player is on the high road to a reasonable degree of skill, with a definite positive guide always at hand, to which he may turn in times of need. He is also on the way to a fuller enjoyment of the game than he has previously known. But this does not mean to say that he has mastered it. For no man has ever become a perfect swinger. By that I mean to say that no one ever has been, or ever will be, able to make a perfect swing at will. He may make ten, twenty, thirty, or more successive strokes with approximate perfection, and yet never have positive assurance that the next will be as good.

Only a machine can perform a mechanical action perfectly, and a machine has no brain, no imagination, and no mental kinks to interfere with its performance. On the other hand, the machine never can, of course, experience the satisfaction that comes from a successful performance, the accomplishment of an objective. I know of few more satisfying experiences than the thrill that comes from conquering the many obstacles involved in developing real skill in playing golf, by one who has known the hard work and worry and anguish that can result from playing badly.

Within reasonable limitations, the degree of skill that one may reasonably expect to develop, once he has learned the art of swinging, will depend largely on intelligent application of the principle he has learned through practice. It is by frequent repetition that any action becomes habitual, that is subconsciously controlled. The great Paderewski is said to have remarked once, "If I miss one day of practice, I can tell it in my playing; if I miss two days in succession, my audience can tell it." I would not go so far as to say that the technique of swinging a golf club is so finely tempered as that, but practice and skillful play are very intimately associated.

Intelligent practice will confirm the player in the performance of the swing and will continually increase the probability that each stroke will approach closer to perfection in performance. What is of even greater importance is constant and continued training in keeping concentration centered on that feeling of the swinging action of the clubhead. The muscular routine can in time be developed to the point where there will be little likelihood of variation, when it functions free of conscious interference. But there can never be any letup on the effort to keep the conscious mind riveted on sensing the feel of the swing.

Reference has already been made to the fact that expert players differ from one another in certain outward appearances. It has likewise been stated that the differences are largely individual mannerisms, which are more or less incidental. In many cases they are the results of an intentional striving for a certain effect; in others they have been developed quite unintentionally. In all cases they serve chiefly to distinguish the individual, even as persons differ one from another in the way they walk.

These differences, however, lead to a consideration of the style and form of different players, or rather to a discussion of these two terms as they relate to golf, since they are widely misunderstood. "I cannot understand," says one, "how it is that Blink plays such a wretched game; he has such a fine style"; or "I don't see how Blank manages to hit the ball at all with that terrible form that he has."

Our hypothetical commentators are merely confused, of course, in their understanding of the two terms. "Form," the dictionary tells us, "is established method of expression or practice." Style is defined as "mode or manner which is deemed elegant, or in accord with a standard; a distinctive or characteristic manner or method."

In other words, form is the capacity for doing a thing in substantially the same way over and over again. If the manner is easy, graceful, and free from the appearance of undue effort, it is good form. Good form appeals to the eye and is style. Style, or the lack of it, so far as golf is concerned, is that which the eye perceives in the performance of others. Form is the player's manner of producing the performance. If, true to the definition, the method of expression or practice is established, it is directed by the sense of feel, and not by sight. Form, however awkward, will produce relatively consistent

*The body turns in swinging, but a swing is not produced by centering attention on the turning. The two figures to the left show reverse body positions when swinging the club with the hands held wide apart; those on the right similar position in swinging the club in the normal way.*

*The top figures show the turn accomplished as the player, with the club held in the arms across the back, seeks to point first one end of the club and then the other at the ball. The purpose is to point the club; the turn is a resulting movement.*

results. Style of performance has no relation to results, except as it indicates good form.

I have introduced this comment here to emphasize once more the folly of trying to copy the mannerisms or styles of other players. It is form alone that counts in building up consistency of performances. Obviously enough, the sounder the form, the more consistent the results obtained. But in any event, efforts to imitate what you see in the bodily actions of another in playing a golf stroke cannot possibly prove of any help to you in discovering the feel of the action that the player himself experiences.

This prompts me to comment briefly on what may profitably be derived from watching expert players in action, and what to look for as they play the stroke. Usually when I am giving a lesson I carry with me a small booklet showing successive stages of the stroke by Bobby Jones. It is arranged in sequence from front to back, and, by flipping the pages between the thumb and forefinger, I can produce the effect of an actual motion picture of the stroke. In calling it to the attention of my pupils, I ask them to watch only the movement of the clubhead and to disregard the body actions. Almost without fail, pupils immediately perceive that the clubhead moves almost as though it were a weight on a string. In other words, within practical limits, the movement is a near-perfect swinging action from first to last.

Therein lies the value in watching the experts in actual play. Observe the steady rhythmic movement of the clubhead, or note the action of the hands in their movement through the stroke. In other words, try to register a picture of the action as a whole, and avoid efforts to pick out single details of this or that position at varying stages of the stroke. The hands hold and control the club. Their movement is directed by the central idea of swinging the clubhead, and succeeding movements of the body, legs, and other parts of the anatomy must be responsive to that one idea.

It should not be necessary to point out that practice, to be of any value whatsoever, must be carried out along sound lines. The mere act of going through the motion accomplishes nothing, unless the player is able to assure himself that the stroke embodies a swinging action. If one has any doubt on this point, the very best thing to do is to get back to the beginning. Try making a short stroke, which requires little turning of the body, and keep at it until you are sure of the feel of the clubhead movement. Then gradually increase the scope of the action. If necessary, go all the way back to swinging a weight on a string through a short arc, as was recommended in an early chapter on how to know and to recognize the swing.

Once you have positively identified the feel of a swing, you will be able to recognize it thereafter, but this does not mean that you will be able to swing smoothly each time you go out to play or take up a club for practice. It may be that after a considerable layoff from play you will find difficulty at first when you try it again. On the other hand, the lapse of a few weeks or so between games may find you returning easily to the routine, when you do play again.

Illustrative of the above point, Miss Virginia Van Wie told me two years ago of an interesting experience she had undergone. Following her winning of the United States Championship at the Whitemarsh Valley Country Club early in October, she played no golf until the following January. During the fall months she did, however, play quite a bit of tennis, requiring quick sharp applications of leverage in the stroke. On her return to golf, her first round was a 95. The following day she began to get back into the routine of swinging, and scored an 86. In her third round, the day after that, she had a 79, marking an improvement of almost a stroke a hole over her first return after the long layoff. I may add that her single purpose in any and all practice sessions is to school her concentration on thinking only of the feeling of the clubhead action.

If this simple plan is sufficient for her, winner of numerous championships, the fact should commend it to the careful consideration of less skillful players.

# −11−

# THE SWING TELLS
# THE STORY

My message from the beginning has been a simple one: "Swing the clubhead." And the reader may recall the warning, sounded in the Foreward, of much repetition. That warning was prompted by the experiences of more than twenty years of practical teaching, and to this day I still find it necessary to go over and over that simple message. Its very simplicity seems to offer the most baffling problem. To some, golf just cannot be that simple. And yet it is. But I have not dared to hope that a presentation of the idea in written form would achieve results more favorable than personal verbal instruction.

There is certainly nothing revolutionary or radical in the idea, but it is something of a variation from the common procedure of teaching the game. As a concession to those who are thoroughly familiar with the usual process of analyzing the stroke piece by piece, in this concluding chapter I propose to show how sound analysis on the above basis is entirely consistent with what has been said of the conception of the stroke as a swinging action.

To do this I have collected quotations from the writings of a number of the notable experts, who have sought to analyze the game for the benefit of others. These I am reproducing here, along with a brief comment on each, pointing out how the theories expressed coincide fully with the swinging idea.

**Robert T. Jones, Jr.:** "The more I play and study golf, the more firmly do I become convinced that the only possibility of a 'grooved' swing lies in the dominant use of the left arm and side. I offer the following six suggestions for developing such a swing.

"1. At the start of the backswing, be certain not to lift the club with the right hand; start back by a push with the left.

"2. Be sure that the hips and shoulders turn freely during the backswing. Do not leave the left heel on the ground.

"3. Keep the left arm extended and do not hug the right elbow in too tightly; allow the right side to be perfectly relaxed as the club is swung back.

"4. Be sure to cock the left wrist at the top of the backswing but hold the club firmly with the left hand, so that it is kept under control.

"5. Hit through with the left arm, and do not discharge the wrist cock too early in the downswing.

"6. Don't be afraid to hit the ball."

Considering the points made in their turn, I have pointed out that the hand on the end of the club must control and guide the action in swinging, even as he points out in his first paragraph, speaking, of course, in terms of the right-handed swinger.

1. Because of its position on the shaft, between the left, which must control, and the head of the club, the right hand must set up a levering process, if it is allowed to set the club head in motion. A stroke started in this way cannot develop a swinging action.

2. Any stroke sufficiently long to require that the clubhead depart from the line running through the objective and the ball makes it necessary for the body to turn to some extent. How much turn takes place is determined by the length of the stroke. For a full stroke, the maximum turn of the body consistent with freedom and comfort will take place, in response to the action of the hands in swinging the clubhead.

3. For practical purposes, the left arm and the shaft of the club are of a piece, establishing the radius of the swing. The expanding action of a swing draws the medium through which the force is being transmitted taut at all times. In golf the left arm is an important section of that medium, and the pull of the swing extends it. Unless the right hand is allowed to interfere by introducing leverage, the right arm will fall naturally and comfortably down by the side as the club is swung back.

4. Flexibility in the wrists permits of the change in direction of the clubhead during the swing. The swinging action, starting slowly and smoothly, is still developing speed at a comparatively slow measure as this change of direction takes place. The increasing speed as the clubhead is swung down to the ball, with an ever-increasing pull by the clubhead at this stage, causes the wrists to react from the bending, which took place in the change of direction, and to contribute to developing maximum speed at impact.

5. The swinging action will cause the left arm to remain extended until after impact. The only way in which the action of the wrist in natural response to a real swing can be hurried is through an effort to inject power into the stroke with the right hand, immediately after the club has changed direction. This, as has been pointed out, means destroying the swing by means of leverage, that is, trying to apply power at some point other than the center.

6. A swing will develop the maximum speed possible with the clubhead from the power that can be properly applied. Efforts to hold back in the application or to turn on more than can be controlled by swinging will interfere with swinging.

**James Braid:** "Generally speaking, iron shots, particularly those played with the shorter irons, are played too quickly, and there is too much hurry at the turning part in the stroke."

Full explanation was made in an early chapter of how a flexing of the wrists makes possible the change in direction of the clubhead, and at the same time retains in the stroke the quality of a swing, from the start until after the ball has been struck. One cannot hurry a swing; the speed of the object being swung can be gradually increased, but not hurried. The actions criticized by Braid are foreign to swinging.

**George Duncan:** "In nearly every case of slicing, the trouble boils down to just this – lack of pivoting."

For anything like a full stroke, it is quite necessary that the body shall turn naturally to allow the hands to swing the clubhead back and upward. This turning will be quite responsive to the hand action, if the stroke is begun as a swing. If the stroke is begun through a levering process, the counter actions of certain sets of muscles

*Another lady champion in action: Lady Heathcote Amory, formerly Miss Joyce Wethered. Here again control of the clubhead*

*through the hands produces a swinging action, with a resultant pull by the clubhead, as contrasted with the use of leverage, which produces a contracting effect.*

against certain others will result in the failure of the body to turn as it should. If the player makes sure of swinging, he need not concern himself in the least about causing the body to turn; that detail will take care of itself.

**Grantland Rice:** "It is the locked body, the tightened body, the lunging body, that does most of the damage in preventing the hands and arms from swinging the clubhead."

The aforementioned conditions in the body result in most cases from a tense condition in starting the swing, due to faulty methods of holding the club, or from a wrong conception of what the player is trying to do, namely, hit the ball with all his might instead of swinging the clubhead, or from conflicting forces in starting the stroke. Swinging demands an easy, relaxed mental and physical condition to begin with. Conditions described in the preceding paragraph cannot develop through swinging.

**Sir Ernest Holderness:** "The fault committed by many golfers is to keep the right knee stiff in starting the club down and on through the stroke, instead of letting it go through with the clubhead."

Even as the left side relaxes in order to permit the body to make an easy turn toward the right in the backward sweep, if the player swings, so the right leg and side relax in the downward and forward sweep, to permit the body to turn easily toward the left. No player who does not introduce leverage into the stroke from the very start, by pulling back with his right hand, will ever experience the trouble of finding his right leg stiff and straight at the knee as the clubhead sweeps down to the ball.

*Action snapshots of Bobby Jones, whose stroke reveals a beautiful rhythmic swinging movement of the clubhead throughout. Note in the lower picture the expanding outward pull of the clubhead, resulting from the swinging force.*

**Miss Joyce Wethered:** "Jerky and uncontrolled movements in which the position of the clubhead is felt to be lost are never included in a fine swing."

The term "swing" has been used here as synonymous with stroke, or movement of the club. A true swinging action can never be jerky, and, as Miss Wethered points out, a feel of where the clubhead is and what is being done with it is present throughout a swing.

**Jerome D. Travers:** "Let the arms pull the body through instead of the body pushing the arms through. This latter is the worst thing in timing."

There is always an outward pull of the clubhead when it is being moved by swinging. What is referred to above as "the body pushing the arms through" means nothing more than that the player is trying to apply power in the wrong way, just as though he tried to increase the speed of a weight being swung on the end of a string by pushing on the string at some intermediate point between the hand and the weight. The futility of such a procedure should be readily evident.

**Horace Hutchinson:** "The right shoulder down and loose, as the club is swung down from the top of the swing, is the first great secret for striking the ball as it should be struck."

So long as the movement retains the nature of a true swing, the left arm will be the guiding agency up to the stage of striking the ball. When this condition obtains, it is quite natural that the right arm and side are comparatively inactive over something like two-thirds of the arc that the hands describe in moving down from their position at the top to that at impact. If the right hand is allowed to inject leverage in starting the downswing, the right shoulder action commended in the preceding paragraph cannot develop.

**Wanda Morgan:** "While I am quite sure that one cannot get length without hitting hard, I am equally sure that hard hitting alone will not produce length."

The distinction here is, of course, the difference explained under Obstacles to Swinging between developing speed to strike the ball hard by swinging and exerting effort to "hit" hard with an application of the power through leverage rather than swinging. One may swing as hard as he can *swing*.

**Grantland Rice:** "You have to time a hit perfectly, whereas a swing will time itself."

A smooth gradual application of power, producing gradual acceleration of clubhead speed is a distinguishing characteristic of swinging. It is extremely difficult to control the application of power through leverage. Leverage is marked by tenseness, and tenseness defies control.

**Gene Sarazen:** "One of the chief essentials of a long straight drive is a brace-up of the left side just before impact."

In a swing the body, turning to the right on the backswing to accommodate the sweep of the arms and hands in carrying the club back and up, finds itself supported chiefly by the right leg at the top of the backswing. Naturally enough, therefore, when moving in the reverse direction during the downswing, the left leg offers the support. The fact that this leg straightens and stiffens just before and during the time the ball is being struck, is merely evidence that the stroke has maintained its swinging action. Any slackening or collapse of the left leg at impact shown that the turning of the body toward the left, in compensation for the necessary turn toward the right in the backswing, has not taken place; therefore, the stroke was not a swing.

**Harry Vardon:** "The upstroke is everything. If it is bad, the downstroke will be wrong, and the ball will not be properly driven."

This is entirely consistent, of course, with the premise that I have set up from the start – that the stroke is a continuous action from start to finish. If it is begun in any manner other than as a swinging action, there is little chance that it will develop into a swing in its later stages. Leverage, employed in starting the action, will prevail throughout.

**Robert T. Jones, Jr.:** "One essential element of the golf stroke, regardless of what path it may take, is a smooth, even acceleration from the top of the swing down to and through the ball."

Throughout these pages I have tried to point out that the only way to obtain a smooth, even acceleration of the speed of the clubhead is through a swinging action.

The foregoing are, I feel, sufficient to point out that intelligent observation and comment on correct methods of wielding the club, viewed from the standpoint of the outward appearances of good players in action, is entirely consistent with the conception of the stroke as a swinging action. As a definite and positive thing that can be identified through feel, swinging therefore offers, to any one who is willing to apply himself to learning it, an open approach to learning to play golf reasonably well.

*Action pictures of two fine lady golfers. Top and bottom, Miss Virginia Van Wie, former United States Champion, at the finish of*

*the stroke and at the limit of the backswing. Both pictures suggest body movement quite free from restraint, in response to swinging the clubhead. Center, Miss Charlotte Glutting just at impact, showing the arms fully extended, as a result of the outward pull by the clubhead exerted through the action of swinging.*

Since the foregoing is true, I am convinced that it is the simplest and easiest way to learn the game, whether one is just taking it up or has been struggling unsuccessfully with it over a period of years. It is for this reason that the reader finds no reference here on how to correct the vast assortment of troubles manifested in efforts to wield the club otherwise than by swinging. Learn to swing, and you have found the high road to good golf.

There remains, however, just one further consideration, involving one bit of advice that is impressed on every golfer – Keep Your Eye on the Ball. To be sure, you look at the ball. If you are trying to strike something with any kind of tool or implement, naturally you look at it. The mere fact that you do look at it will not insure that you strike it as you intend. Doubtless the reader has had experiences in driving a nail or tack with a hammer which qualify him to give testimony to this fact. But looking at it helps just the same.

But remember this. No more conscious effort to look at the ball is needed in striking a golf ball than in driving a nail. We look at the nail as a matter of course, and we continue to look at it if we experience no impulse to turn the gaze elsewhere. It will be just as easy to look at the golf ball while we are striking it, if we can keep out attention from wandering. The surest way to prevent a distraction is to direct conscious attention to sensing a feel of the action of the clubhead.

On the other hand, if we consider looking at the ball as a definite thing that we are required to do, this fact in itself will tend to distract the attention from sensing that feel of the clubhead action. I have seen players so intent on making sure that they "kept the eye on the ball" during a stroke that they completely lost sight of the important matter of striking the ball. Look at the ball, but do not make a ceremony of it. Almost any good player can hit the ball as far and as straight with his eyes shut as he can with them open, once he has taken up his position and addressed the ball. Like other attendant actions, the practice of looking at the ball will become entirely responsive, once the player has developed the routine of making a smooth, rhythmic swing.

In conclusion, let me remark once more that good golf is easy – easy to play and enjoyable. As Bobby Jones has remarked, "Correct use of the muscles of the body contributes great power, and easily controlled power, too. Incorrect use of them is entirely hopeless." Swinging is the easiest and simplest method of applying controlled power.

## Swing the Clubhead!

52263160R00066

Made in the USA
San Bernardino, CA
06 September 2019